Countries
on the
World Stage

SPOTLIGHT ON

the United States

Tracy Sue Walker

Lerner Publications ◆ Minneapolis

Content consultants: Jill Doerfler and Cleopatra Warren, PhD, Atlanta Public Schools

Lerner Publications Company
An imprint of Lerner Publishing Group, Inc.
241 First Avenue North
Minneapolis, MN 55401 USA

For reading levels and more information, look up this title at www.lernerbooks.com.

Main body text set in Aptifer Sans LT Pro Semibold.
Typeface provided by Linotype AG.

Designer: Athena Currier
Lerner team: Martha Kranes, Sue Marquis

Library of Congress Cataloging-in-Publication Data

Names: Walker, Tracy Sue, author.
Title: Spotlight on the United States / Tracy Sue Walker.
Description: Minneapolis : Lerner Publications, 2024. | Series: Countries on the world stage |
    Includes bibliographical references. | Audience: Ages 8–12 | Audience: Grades 4–6 |
    Summary: "The United States is a superpower whose influence reaches far beyond its
    borders. Learn about how the country's past shapes its present. Then discover the US's
    economy, government, and key leaders"— Provided by publisher.
Identifiers: LCCN 2022042910 (print) | LCCN 2022042911 (ebook) | ISBN 9781728492049
    (library binding) | ISBN 9798765602607 (paperback) | ISBN 9781728496788 (ebook)
Subjects: LCSH: United States—Juvenile literature.
Classification: LCC E178.3 .W239 2024 (print) | LCC E178.3 (ebook) | DDC 973—dc23/
    eng/20220912

LC record available at https://lccn.loc.gov/2022042910
LC ebook record available at https://lccn.loc.gov/2022042911

Manufactured in the United States of America
1-53143-51153-1/5/2023

TABLE OF CONTENTS

INTRODUCTION

Declaration of Independence

BRITISH COLONISTS MET ON A HOT SUMMER DAY IN PHILADELPHIA, PENNSYLVANIA. They were deciding if they wanted to remain British subjects or form their own nation. Benjamin Franklin, John Adams, and other colonists carefully read Thomas Jefferson's Declaration of Independence.

The colonists decided to continue fighting a war with Britain to have their own country. On August 2, 1776, the colonists signed Jefferson's document. It was the beginning of a new nation, the United States of America.

By signing the Declaration of Independence, colonists declared their freedom from Britain.

First Peoples and the First World War

For thousands of years, Indigenous peoples lived on the land that became the United States. There were hundreds of nations. Each had a unique culture. But in the 1500s, European colonists came. They said they discovered the land even though people already lived there. The colonists set up places to live. They forced Indigenous peoples to leave where they had been. But many Indigenous peoples fought back. Some Indigenous peoples fled west to be safe from colonists' attacks.

The Pueblo people finished building Pueblo Bonito in 1150. The cultural site is located in present-day New Mexico.

INDIGENOUS PEOPLES TODAY

In modern times, there are almost six hundred Indigenous nations in the United States. This means members are citizens of three different governments—their nation, the state where they live, and the United States. These nations play an essential role in protecting the varied cultures and identities of Native peoples. They also protect the welfare and safety of their citizens within their nations' territories.

Starting in the sixteenth century, white enslavers kidnapped Black people from Africa and brought them to the Americas. The enslavers forced Black people into slavery in the American colonies and in countries such as Britain and Brazil. More than twelve million Black people were kidnapped and forced to go to North America, the Caribbean, and South America over three hundred years. Enslaved Black people

Enslavers used ships to transport Black people to North America and other areas against their will.

This painting shows George Washington (*center*) fighting in the Revolutionary War (1775–1783).

worked without pay. Many worked on large farms, mostly in the South. They grew important crops such as cotton and tobacco. Other enslaved people were unpaid construction workers, craftspeople, and household workers. In this way, enslaved Black people created much of the region's wealth.

As more Europeans immigrated, some colonists wanted to be separate from England. They didn't think it was fair that they paid taxes for goods from England but had no say in their government.

England wanted to keep the colonies, so the two sides fought in the Revolutionary War. The colonies won their independence. But only wealthy white men had the freedom to vote in the new country.

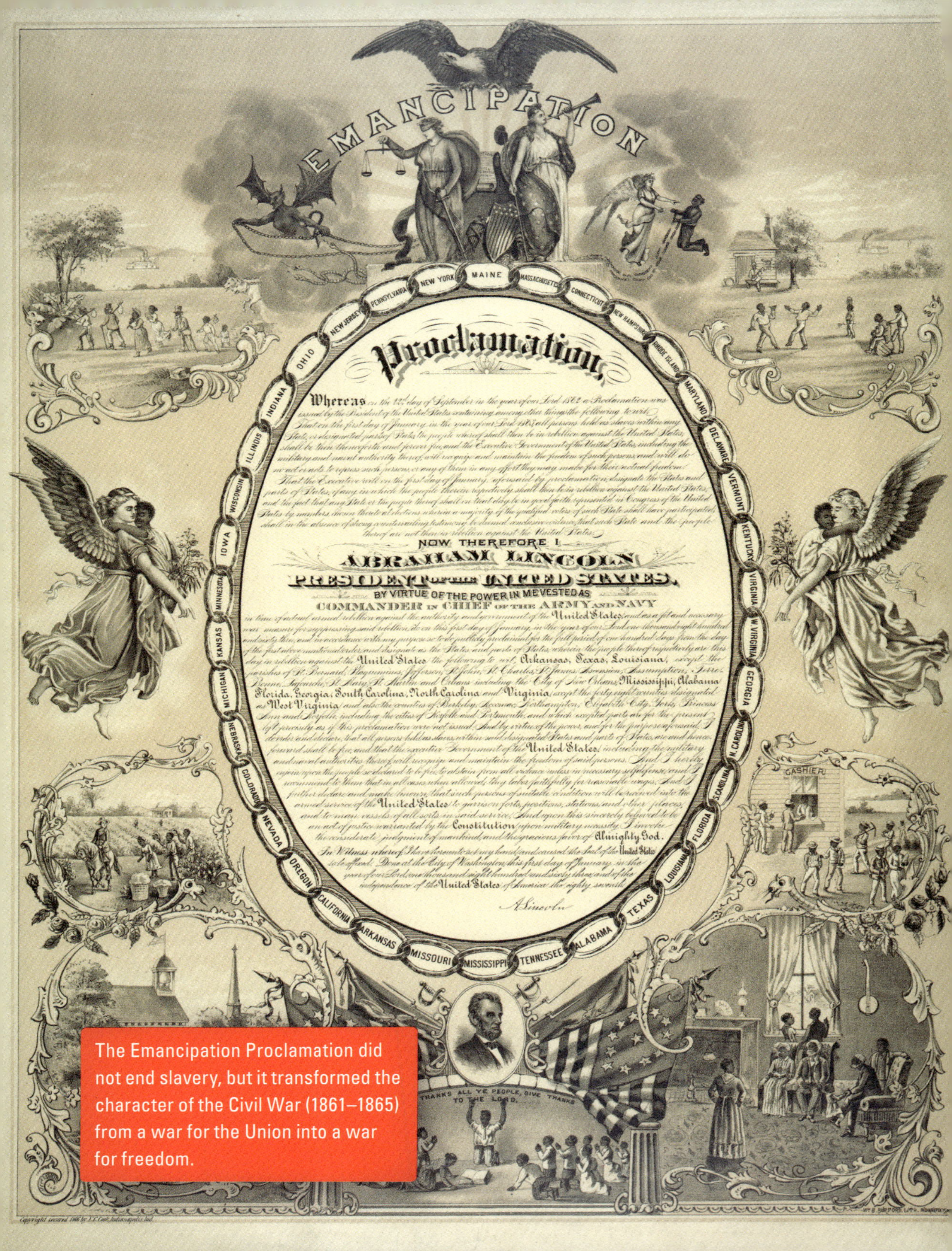

The Emancipation Proclamation did not end slavery, but it transformed the character of the Civil War (1861–1865) from a war for the Union into a war for freedom.

In 1861 the United States went to war with itself in the Civil War. The Northern states and Southern states fought over slavery. The North wanted to end slavery, while the South wanted to keep it. In 1863 President Abraham Lincoln issued the Emancipation Proclamation. This declared that enslaved people in the states that were under the South's control were free. It wasn't until June 19, 1865, that all enslaved people in the South learned of their freedom. Each year, people celebrate freedom on Juneteenth with parades, cookouts, and more.

About fifty years after the Civil War, in 1917, the United States entered World War 1 (1914–1918). The United States joined several nations, the Allies, to fight against Germany, Austria-Hungary, Bulgaria, and the Ottoman Empire. The Allies won the war.

US soldiers fight in the trenches of World War I.

CHAPTER 2

Landscapes and Citizens

Covering almost 3.8 million square miles (9.8 million sq. km), the United States is the world's fourth-largest country. It is located on the continent of North America. Mexico lies south of it and Canada is to its north. The country is divided into regions based on similar natural and cultural features. Those regions are the Northeast, Southwest, West, Southeast, and Midwest.

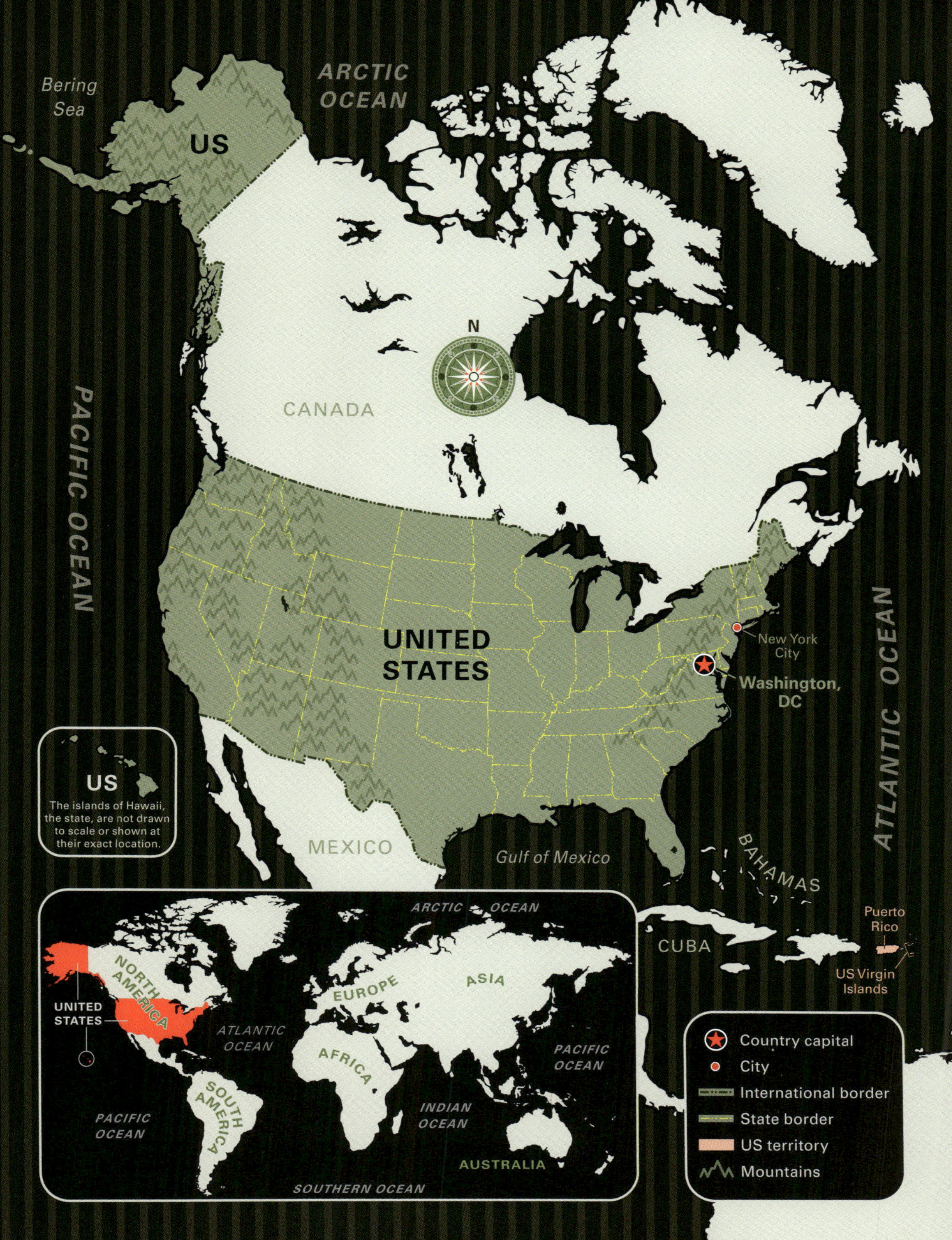

Bering Sea
ARCTIC OCEAN
US
PACIFIC OCEAN
CANADA
N
UNITED STATES
New York City
Washington, DC
ATLANTIC OCEAN
US
The islands of Hawaii, the state, are not drawn to scale or shown at their exact location.
MEXICO
Gulf of Mexico
BAHAMAS
Puerto Rico
CUBA
US Virgin Islands
NORTH AMERICA
UNITED STATES
EUROPE
ASIA
ATLANTIC OCEAN
AFRICA
PACIFIC OCEAN
INDIAN OCEAN
SOUTH AMERICA
PACIFIC OCEAN
AUSTRALIA
SOUTHERN OCEAN
Country capital
City
International border
State border
US territory
Mountains

EXPLORE US TERRITORIES

In addition to states, the US also has sixteen territories such as Puerto Rico, Guam, and the US Virgin Islands. People living in these territories are US citizens, but they have different rights than citizens of states. They elect nonvoting delegates to represent them in the US Congress. They are not allowed to vote for president. Similarly, residents of Washington, DC, the nation's capital, also send nonvoting delegates to the US Congress. But citizens from DC have the right to vote for president.

The country borders the Pacific Ocean to the west and the Atlantic Ocean to the east. The beaches and clay of the South turn into the rolling plains of the Midwest, where crops such as corn and soybeans grow. Those plains rise into the mountain

The US grows about fourteen billion bushels of corn and four billion bushels of soybeans a year. A bushel equals 8 gallons (36 L).

peaks of the West and the desert sands of the Southwest.
Many beef farms and ranches are found in the Southwest and
West. People fish off the coasts of the Northeast.

More than 331 million people call the United States home.
Over the past few decades, there has been an increase in
racial and ethnic diversity in the country. This diversity creates
exchanges of ideas and traditions that make the country
stronger. Currently, about 60 percent of the population is
white, and about 19 percent is Latino. Black Americans make
up around 14 percent of the population. About 6 percent of
the population is of Asian descent, while Native Americans and
Alaska Natives make up just over 1 percent.

CHAPTER 3

Becoming a World Power

The US economy boomed in the 1920s.
After the period of growth, the stock market crashed in October 1929. People and businesses lost a lot of money, which led to economic problems for the whole country. Many Americans lost their jobs and homes. The time was called the Great Depression (1929–1939), and it impacted countries around the globe.

The Depression ended during World War II (1939–1945). The war began when Adolf Hitler and Germany's Nazi Party invaded Poland in September 1939. The Nazis used people's anger over the economy to spread hatred of and promote violence against groups of people, especially Jewish people. The United States joined the war in 1941. It helped a group of countries called the Allies defeat Germany, Japan, and Italy. After the war, the United States used its victory and industrial might to become a world superpower.

People wait to receive free soup during the Great Depression.

The modern United States has the world's largest economy. But the country also has a large wealth gap. This means the richest US citizens, a small percentage of the population, own most of the country's wealth.

New York City's Financial District is home to many banks and other financial businesses.

Service industries make up the largest portion of the US economy. These services include financial, health care, entertainment, travel, retail, and more.

The United States is the world's largest importer of goods and services. Some of the country's top exports are cars and gas. Agricultural goods, manufacturing, and services are all traded by the United States.

Constitution and Branches

The United States is a republic. Its government is run by elected officials. Citizens who are eighteen years old or older can vote. States have different voting laws, and in some states people convicted of felony crimes are not allowed to vote. Voters elect people to represent them at city, county, state, and federal levels.

The US Constitution created the country's government system. It was written by a group of leaders from the first thirteen states in the 1780s. It was meant to make sure the

The US Constitution is on permanent display at the National Archives Museum in Washington, DC.

government could act on a national level and still protect people's individual rights. The Constitution was inspired by both European and Indigenous thinkers. At that time, only wealthy white men had full citizenship rights, so women and people of color weren't protected by the Constitution.

The Constitution also created three branches of government. Congress, the legislative branch, makes the laws. People of each state and territory elect delegates to represent them in Congress. The executive branch enforces the laws and includes the president, vice president, cabinet, and federal agencies. The judicial branch evaluates the laws and includes the Supreme Court and lower courts.

Separate branches of government ensure that one branch doesn't become too powerful. They check one another's power. The legislative branch is made up of the House of Representatives and the Senate, representing fifty states. Congress has the power to introduce a bill that might become law. The president may veto bills or sign them into

POLITICAL PARTIES

The United States has political parties. Political parties are groups that try to win elections and influence the government. Some of the country's founders worried that political parties would cause conflict in government. However, by the presidential election of 1796, political parties were already in place. Currently, the most powerful US political parties are the Democratic and Republican Parties.

law. Supreme Court justices are appointed by the president and confirmed by the Senate. Justices serve for their life or until they retire. Members of Congress and the president are elected to terms. The president can serve up to two four-year terms. Members of the Senate serve six-year terms, and members of the House of Representatives have two-year

Representatives in the House vote on an act in 2022.

Vice President Kamala Harris (*right*) swears Deb Haaland (*with hand raised*) into office as secretary of the interior in 2021.

terms. Members of Congress can run for reelection as many times as they choose.

In 2020 Joe Biden was elected president of the United States. Biden had a groundbreaking administration. Kamala Harris was the first woman, first Black person, and first Asian American to serve as vice president. Harris presides over the Senate. Secretary of Transportation Pete Buttigieg, the first openly gay cabinet member, is working to improve the nation's public transportation systems. Deb Haaland was the first Native American to serve as secretary of the interior. She focuses on shaping environmentally friendly business practices.

The US in Modern Times

THE UNITED STATES IS A GLOBAL POWER, BUT IT ALSO FACES CHALLENGES. Climate change threatens the nation with wildfires, droughts, extreme storms, and more. The United States will have to figure out how to address these problems. The country can lessen the impacts of climate change by using renewable energy sources, such as wind and water.

People protest against racial inequality after the murder of George Floyd by a police officer in 2020.

Racial equity is another concern facing the country. On May 25, 2020, George Floyd, a Black man, was murdered in Minneapolis, Minnesota. A white police officer named Derek Chauvin pressed his knee on Floyd's neck, killing him. This event highlighted racism throughout the United States. Millions of people around the country protested for racial justice. A bill to address policing problems around the country was named after Floyd, but it hasn't passed the legislative branch. Racism is still a major challenge for the United States.

Many people in the United States struggle to pay for health care and education. This means that some people can't afford to see a doctor or go to college. New laws could help fix these issues, but they would need to pass Congress and be signed into law by the president. Even with these challenges, the United States is a rich, diverse country and world leader. It will remain a world power well into the future.

President Biden (*center*) signs a bill into law that limits how much some people pay for insulin medication.

TIMELINE

ca. 15,000 BCE	The first peoples arrive in the area that is now the United States.
1500s CE	British colonists arrive in North America and create colonies.
1776	The Declaration of Independence is written and signed during the Revolutionary War.
1861–1865	The Civil War is fought between the North and South over the future of slavery in the United States.
1865	By June 19, all enslaved people in the South had learned of their freedom. The day is celebrated every year as Juneteenth.
1929–1939	The Great Depression causes millions of people in the US and around the world to lose their jobs and homes.
1941–1945	The United States fights in World War II against the Axis powers.
2020	Millions of people in the United States protest against racial inequality after George Floyd is murdered by a white police officer. Joe Biden is elected president.
2022	The US Supreme Court overturns the *Roe v. Wade* decision, ending the constitutional right to an abortion.

UNITED STATES FAST FACTS

Name: United States of America

Population: 333,011,087

Land area: 3,796,742 square miles (9,833,517 sq. km)

Largest city: New York City

Capital city: Washington, DC

Form of government: democratic republic

Official language: no official language; over 350 different languages spoken in the US, with English spoken by the majority and Spanish as the next most common language

Flag:

GLOSSARY

citizen: a person who legally belongs to a country and has the rights and protection of that country

culture: the beliefs, social practices, and characteristics of a particular society or group

delegate: a person who is chosen or elected to vote or act for others

equity: fairness or justice in the way people are treated

ethnic: relating to races or large groups of people who have the same customs, religion, and origin

export: to send a product to be sold in another country

racism: poor treatment of or violence against people because of their race

right: something that a person is or should be morally or legally allowed to have, get, or do

veto: the power of a government official to keep something from taking effect

LEARN MORE

Britannica Kids: Racism
https://kids.britannica.com/kids/article/racism/632495

Britannica Kids: United States Constitution
https://kids.britannica.com/kids/article/United-States-Constitution
/353886

Doerfler, Jill, and Matthew J. Martinez. *Deb Haaland: First Native American Cabinet Secretary*. Minneapolis: Lerner Publications, 2023.

Gordon, Sharon, and Jennifer Lombardo. *United States*. Buffalo: Cavendish Square, 2023.

Hansen, Grace. *Kamala Harris: First Female Vice President of the United States*. Minneapolis: Abdo Kids, 2022.

Kids in the House: How Laws Are Made
https://kids-clerk.house.gov/grade-school/lesson.html?intID=17

Kopp, Megan. *United States*. New York: Lightbox Learning, 2021.

National Geographic Kids: United States
https://kids.nationalgeographic.com/geography/countries/article
/united-states

INDEX

PHOTO ACKNOWLEDGMENTS

Image credits: Matt Champlin/Getty Images, p. 7; National Archives and Records Administration, pp. 5, 21; Library of Congress, pp. 8, 10; Courtesy of the Doe Memorial Library via Wikimedia Commons, p. 9; Everett Collection/Shutterstock.com, p. 11; LKW/IPS, p. 13; oticki/Shutterstock.com, p. 14; James Andrews1/Shutterstock.com, p. 15; Science History Images/Alamy Stock Photo, p. 17; Alexander Spatari/Getty Images, p. 18; bfk92/Getty Images, p. 19; Fred Schilling, Collection of the Supreme Court of the United States; Chip Somodevilla/Getty Images, p. 23; AP Photo/Alex Brandon, p. 24; Ira L. Black/Corbis/Getty Images, p. 26; AP Photo/Yuri Gripas/Abaca/Sipa USA, p. 27; charnsitr/Shutterstock.com, p. 29.

Cover: Kevin Voelker Photography/Getty Images.